Doozandohn

Illustrated guide to
Being Popular

Published by Top That! Publishing plc
Copyright © 2010 Top That! Publishing plc
Tide Mill Way, Woodbridge, Suffolk, IP12 1AP, UK
www.topthatpublishing.com
Top That! is a registered trademark of Top That! Publishing plc
All rights reserved

This edition published in Great Britain in 2010 by Top That! Publishing plc,
Marine House, Tide Mill Way,
Woodbridge, Suffolk, IP12 1AP, UK
www.topthatpublishing.com
0 2 4 6 8 9 7 5 3 1

Creative Director – Simon Couchman
Editorial Director – Daniel Graham
Art Editor – Matt Denny

Written and illustrated by Andrew Pinder

All rights reserved. No part of this publication may be reproduced, stored in a retrieval system, or transmitted in any form or by any means, electronic, mechanical, photocopying, recording or otherwise, without the prior written permission of the publisher. Neither this book nor any part or any of the illustrations, photographs or reproductions contained in it shall be sold or disposed of otherwise than as a complete book, and any unauthorised sale of such part illustration, photograph or reproduction shall be deemed to be a breach of the publisher's copyright.

ISBN 978-1-84956-080-1

A catalogue record for this book is available from the British Library
Printed and bound in China

This is a work of fiction. Names, characters, places, incidents and dialogues are products of the author's imagination or are used fictitiously. Any resemblance to actual people, living or dead, events or locales is entirely coincidental.

Foreword

Why are some people effortlessly popular? By contrast, other people, no matter how hard they try, never gain the same level of respect. Following years of painstaking research, at the Top That! Institute of Behavioural Studies, I have solved the complex social equation of how to become popular and stay that way. Now, YOU can reap the benefits of my studies by reading this learnamologically enhanced book.

During my research, I learnt that humour is one of the most important component parts of popularity. History provides countless examples of unelected world leaders, who lacked the ability to appreciate humour and, as a result, were always unpopular. That is why I have teamed up with the world's best doodle artist, Andrew Pinder, and have presented my findings as simple 'Do' and 'Don't' instructions, with a life-enriching dollop of humour. As the saying goes, if you laugh, then the world laughs with you, and if the world is with you, then you're already well on the way to being popular.

I hope that you enjoy reading my findings, and that they help you to make decisions, which lead to a happier lifestyle.

A cautionary note:

Reading and acting upon the advice contained in this book may have side effects. During trials, a high percentage of my test subjects experienced a rapid deterioration in their number of free weekends, due to social commitments. Other members of my testing team experienced minor levels of fatigue as a direct result of new sports and activities that they had taken up during the trials.

Dr Heinz Doozandohntz

DO be modest about your achievements.

DON'T overdo the modesty.
If you've done something good, you deserve some praise!

DO take up a team sport – it can make you very popular.

DON'T choose a sport that you're useless at – it can make you very unpopular!

Gooaaal!!!

That's our end, fat-head!

DO your brilliant impersonation of the school bully.

DON'T do it when he's around.

DO take an interest in the latest fashions. It's good to keep up.

DON'T become a 'fashion victim'.

DO buy clothes that make you stand out.

DON'T go too far, or you'll look like a freak.

DO choose friends that have similar interests to you.

DON'T think that you can be popular with everyone.

Sporty Geek Thug Goth Posh Political

JUST STOP IT NOW!

DO be a good listener.

DON'T be a gossip and pass on what you have been told.

DO try and look pleasant. Smile!

DON'T smile all of the time – sometimes it is just not appropriate.

DO learn a musical instrument.

DO be amusing and witty in class.

DON'T confuse wit with cheek.
Cheek might get you a bigger laugh, but the consequences are far less beneficial.

DO prepare witty replies for when someone is rude to you.

Like, whatever Trevor!

DON'T try them on:

a. a teacher

b. the school bully

Ow!

DO take up a hobby — being interested in something makes you interesting.

BUILD A ROBOT KIT

DON'T choose a hobby that might scare people off.

A GUIDE TO STUFFING THINGS

THE YOUNG TAXIDERMIST

DO learn to cook.

DON'T be shy. Share your yummy home cooking.

DO be proud of your interests, whether you're a rugby player or a ballet dancer.

DON'T forget that there are a million ways to be cool.

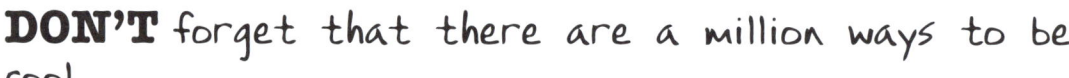

Cool video game player · Cool hamster trainer · Cool stamp collector · Cool carpenter · Cool rider · Cool cook

DO be prepared to stand out from the crowd and be different.

DON'T stand out from the crowd too much.

DO start a band. Nothing could be cooler.

DON'T do it, unless you have the instruments and can play them. Nothing could be sadder.

DO stand in the spotlight. Do public speaking, act, play, sing, and get noticed!

DON'T hog the spotlight. No one likes a show-off!

DO do something new. Join a club and learn a cool new sport.

Kendo

Rock climbing

Karate

Caving

Free running

Scuba diving

Or, if that doesn't interest you, learn a new craft.

Pottery

Sculpting

Metal work

Painting

It's a great way to meet new people.

DON'T participate in extreme sports on your own – it can be dangerous.

DO get permission from your parents before you take up a new club, sport or craft.

DO see if you can volunteer for some outdoor work in the holidays – it could be helping on a conservation project ...

... or working to clean up a beauty spot

DO see if you can help out collecting for a charity – you'll meet loads of new people, all of whom will think that you're saintly and lovely.

DON'T be too aggressive in your collecting techniques – you don't want to ruin your image.

DO try to be pleasant to everyone. If there is someone you can't stand, just avoid them.

DON'T ever bully. Bullies are not respected, not liked and are not popular. They are feared, which is not nearly as good.

DO stick with what you feel to be right.

DON'T get talked into doing things that you know to be wrong, in order to be more popular.

DO throw great parties – you'll soon be popular.

DON'T expect to be very popular with your parents.

DO help others who aren't good at a subject by explaining it.

DON'T do their homework for them, however hard they try and persuade you.

DO the best you can at school.

DON'T copy the mouthy student at the back of the class. He might be popular now ...

... but he won't look so cool in a few years' time.

DO make the best of yourself, but don't worry too much about your looks. You don't have to be perfect to be popular.

DON'T forget Quasimodo – he was ugly and popular...

... actually, come to think about it, the book was popular, he wasn't.

Best not use him as a role model.

DO try and keep in shape – it will make you feel better about yourself.

DON'T get obsessed and become a fitness bore.

DO be a bit of a chameleon.

You have to change how you act depending on who you're with.

DON'T change your whole personality and put on an act ... ... you won't know whether you're coming or going.

DON'T be too much of a chameleon!

DO be generous, nobody likes a miser.

DON'T try to buy popularity – it will only last as long as your sweets.

DO, by all means, buy the newest cool gadget, if you can afford it.

DON'T think that it will make you more popular.

DO something ...

go for a walk, or a run, or hang out with friends, practise sport,

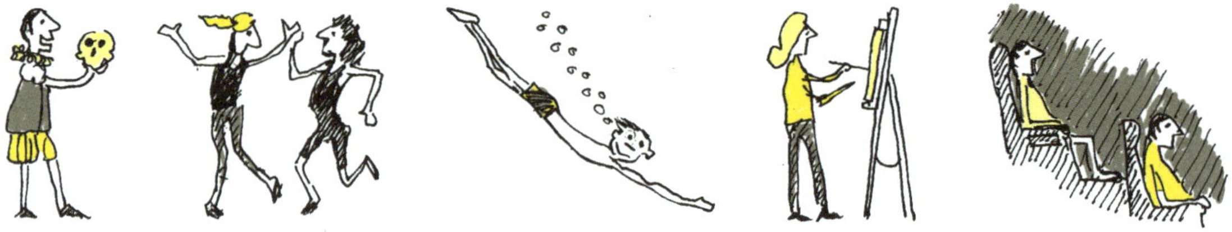

act, dance, swim,  join an archaeological dig, garden, phone a friend ...

DON'T vegetate, nobody gets popular lying on a sofa.

I am afraid that your son has grown into the sofa

DO organise days out with your friends.

DON'T just sit by the telephone waiting for someone else to do it.

DO just be yourself.

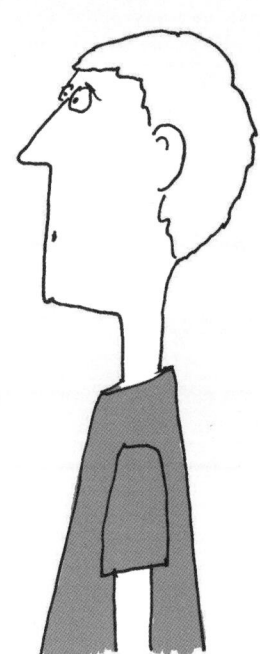

DON'T put on an act – you won't be able to keep it up.

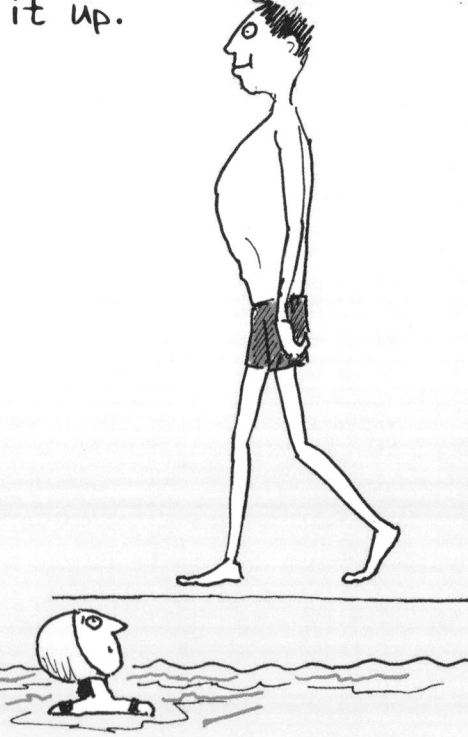

DO what you want to do, even if it makes you look a bit eccentric.

DON'T forget that there is a fine line between interestingly eccentric, and downright mad.

DO have a sense of humour about yourself – everyone has embarrassing accidents, so learn to laugh at them.

DON'T get cross when something happens. If you laugh other people won't laugh at you.

N.B. You don't have to do this if you have been badly hurt.

DO always own up when you have an accident.

DON'T always blame your baby brother or the dog.

DO eat healthily and keep clean, but ...

... **DON'T** get obsessive about the occasional skin blemish. Nobody ever became unpopular because of the odd spot.

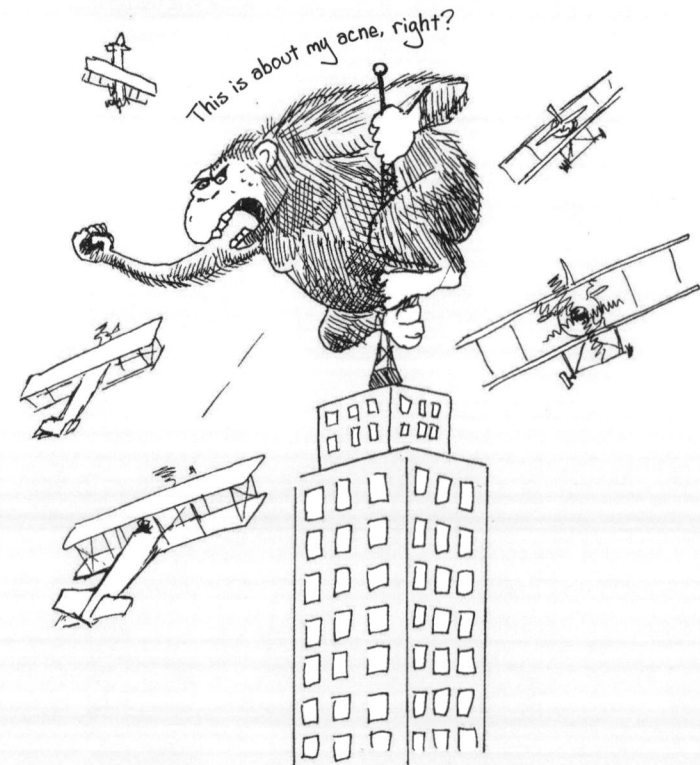

This is about my acne, right?

DO try not to be too shy. Shy people are not unpopular, it is just that nobody notices them. Be brave and join in.

DON'T be so extrovert that you become a pain.

DO walk away from fights if you possibly can.

Oi, you've got a fat head!

Yeah, yeah, fattest one in the school.

Yep, that is a fat head!

DON'T get into stupid scraps – it won't impress anyone, except the very dimwitted.

DO think what it means to be popular. You might know somebody with 1500 friends on Facebook ...

DON'T be fooled – they probably just don't get out enough.

To sum up: to be popular you **DON'T** have to be ...

 ... rich

 ... good looking

 ... super fit

 ... funny all the time.

DON'T ...

 ... be aggressive

 ... boast

 ... gossip

 ... be mean

... vegetate

 ... worry too much about it.

DO remember that being popular, and always having to be cool, can actually be quite lonely ...

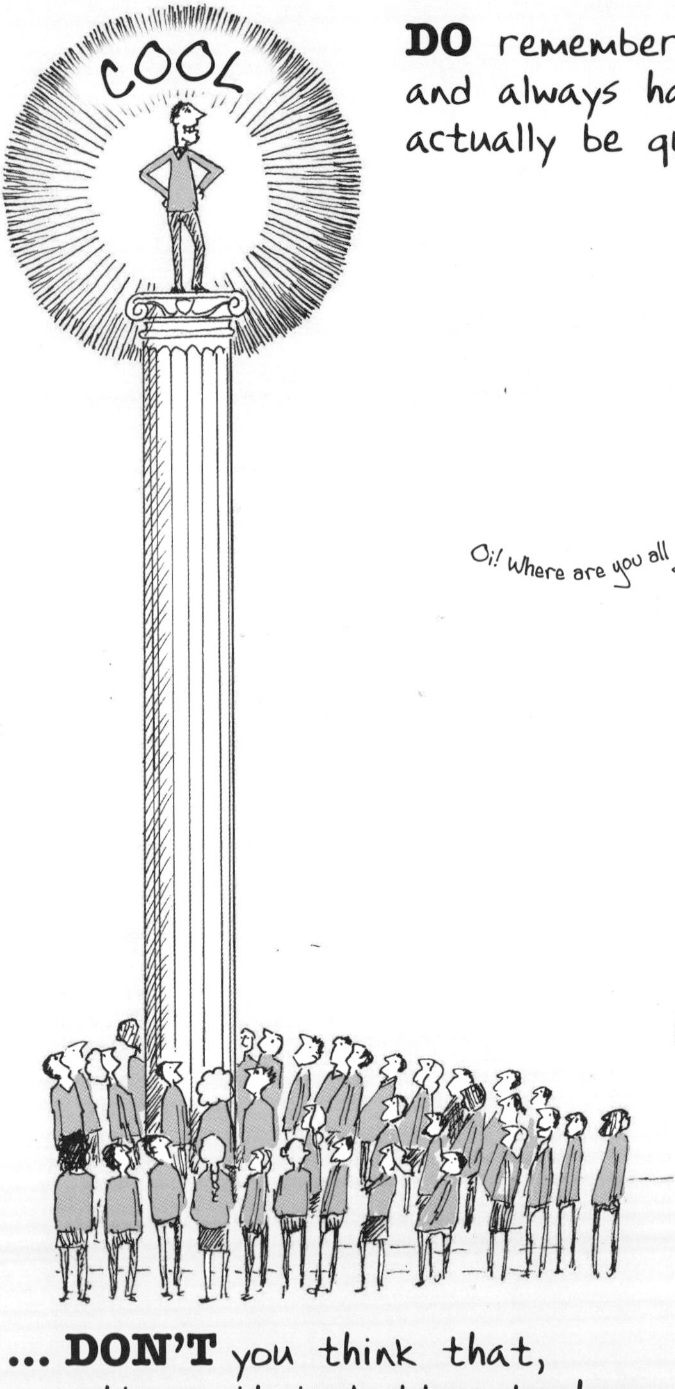

... **DON'T** you think that, sometimes, it is better to have three or four close friends?